IN THIS TEMPLE:

THE STORY OF HENRY BACON

CREATOR OF THE LINCOLN MEMORIAL

Paul Woodbury

The Publishing Laboratory
University of North Carolina at Wilmington

Published by the Publishing Laboratory
The University of North Carolina at Wilmington
601 South College Road
Wilmington North Carolina, 28403-3297

First Edition

Henry Bacon, Jr.
1866 - 1924

Dedication

It seems ironic that the Lincoln Memorial is one of the most well-known and revered landmarks in our nation, yet the man who designed and built it, Henry Bacon, never received the fame that should have been his. To the memory of this Wilmingtonian, then, I dedicate this story.

Acknowledgements

In the course of researching this story, I was aided immeasureably by Philip Furia, of the University of North Carolina at Wilmington. Hopefully I have sucessfully met his criteria to seek out and honestly describe the real person.

I also thank Dr. Rush Bender and Merle Chamberlain, who labor with love in the archives of the Historical Society of the Lower Cape Fear, for their warm help and advice.

Likewise, my deep appreciation to the staff of the North Carolina Room of the New Hanover County Library for their assistance, and also to Wilmington's dean of practicing architects, William F. Boney for his steadfast promotion of Bacon's memory.

Finally, my thanks to Dr. Stanley Colbert for his encouragement in this project and to Neil Smith for his guidance in the craft.

It was warm the evening of May 18, 1923. The earlier rain had not dampened the spirits of the crowd gathered at the reflecting pool at the west end of Potomac Park in Washington, DC. The celebration had started at 6:30 with dinner under a marquee on the grounds at the east end of the pool. Now, dressed in bright robes and waving banners, the celebrants lined the torch-lit, rectangular waterway, giving the scene the air of a medieval pageant. At the far end of the pool, the Lincoln Memorial, awash in colored lights and blurred by lingering mists, appeared magical. The atmosphere was one of anticipation and excitement. At precisely 9:00 p.m., Henry Bacon, architect, accompanied by William B. Faville, President of the American Institute of Architects, embarked on a small barge which awaited them at the east end of the pool.

Bacon stood self-confident in the center of the craft. He appeared aloof and statuesque as the barge moved slowly, pulled by the architectural students who lined the sides of pool. Gently, the craft stopped against the pool edge in front of the broad steps leading up to the Lincoln Memorial. Inside, the nineteen-foot high statue of Abraham Lincoln seemed to look down on the panorama. Bacon stepped deliberately ashore and was escorted up the stairs by the former president, Chief Justice William H. Taft, to the platform where the President of the United States, Warren G. Harding, waited. Harding, like the thousands of onlookers, was there to honor Henry Bacon and to praise Bacon's last and greatest work, the Lincoln Memorial.

The architect from Wilmington, North Carolina, was famous. Although nobody suspected it at the time, this ceremony at the Lincoln Memorial also marked the culmination of Bacon's career. Nine months after the ceremony, Henry Bacon, creator of the Lincoln Memorial, was dead.

Born in Wateka, Illinois in 1866, the year following the end of the Civil War and Lincoln's assassination, Bacon was just one-year old when the U.S. Congress first authorized the creation of a memorial to Abraham Lincoln. Bacon's father, a respected railroad engineer, was caught up in the national rush to extend the rail networks, and family life was nomadic as he moved from job to job. In 1876, when Henry was ten, his father accepted a challenge from the US Army Corps of Engineers and they moved to Smithville, North Carolina (now Southport) where Henry Bacon, Senior, turned his skills to harnessing the Cape Fear River.

Bacon's mother held the family together during those years. To her fell the tasks of packing, moving, cooking, cleaning, caring for five children, and serving as their teacher. Elizabeth Kelton Bacon, a former schoolteacher and a daughter of an old Lexington Massachusetts family, proved herself capable. Still, it must have been a relief to her when, after twenty years of chasing railroads, the family finally settled in North Carolina.

To avoid confusing him with his father, young Henry Junior, was nicknamed "Harry" by family members and friends. Home-schooled by his mother during his early years, Bacon also learned by observing his father. He made frequent outings to his father's project site and watched as his father directed the construction. Here he saw the cool impersonal manner with which his father managed the work and workers. As his later work demonstrated, Harry learned well his father's early lessons about attention to detail, professional integrity, and inflexibility in construction standards. Photographs of his father at work on the Cape Fear River opposite Southport show that the elder Bacon was inflexible in appearance. He was invariably clothed authoritatively in dark suit and vest, wearing a black bowler hat, with hands clasped behind his back as he watched authoritatively over the work in progress. Proud, even magisterial looking, he had a full white beard and looked a lot like General Robert E. Lee. As young Henry matured, he emulated these traits and grew rock steady in his singleness of purpose and inflexibility.

In 1880, at age 14, Bacon left his family and moved upriver to the port city of Wilmington to study at Tileston Normal School. The next year he went to Boston to study at the Chauncey Hall School, but returned in 1882 and graduated with honors from Tileston on May 30, 1884. Following Bacon's death, his former teacher at Tileston, Miss Atta Nutter, remembered her former student, Harry, in a letter to his sister: "His imagination led his fingers. There was little useless expression. A brief, neat, orderly solution he would present or nothing. At times he seemed pugnacious, so persistent was his thought." She wrote on, "Clear vision was his...he seemed to know instinctively what was worth while. His course was direct in life. He made no useless detours. The principles for which he stood at death were his at birth, I do believe." Mrs. Nutter closed with this thought: "Poets are born, it is said, not made. Perhaps this is true of those whose imagination is expressed in stone."

We don't know why Bacon chose to become an architect, but it seems likely that the public buildings and large mansions being constructed in Wilmington while he lived there may have influenced his decision. So, following his graduation from Tileston in 1884, Bacon left home to study architecture at Illinois Industrial University (now the University of Illinois) at Urbana. However, at the suggestion of his older brother, Francis, he dropped out of college after just one year and went to work as an apprentice for the Boston architectural firm of Chamberlain and Whidden in order to gain eligibility for the prestigious Rotch Traveling Scholarship, awarded by the Boston Society of Architects. In May 1888, as soon as he became eligible for the scholarship, Bacon left Chamberlain and Whidden and joined the prestigious architectural firm of McKim, Mead, and White in New York.

In the 1880s, American architecture was at a crossroads. The Great Chicago Fire of 1871 had created the need for major re-building. That same year in New York, the first building with an elevator was completed. This new invention, coupled with the new steel products and alloys, made sky-scrapers a possibility. In Europe, led by the Icole des Beaux-Arts in Paris, the profession abandoned the Traditional and Italianate, the studied mixing of styles, and experimented with a new modernism epitomized in the Eiffel Tower. A strong new voice in American architecture, Louis Sullivan and a young unknown, Frank Lloyd Wright, argued that America should join this movement. The promise of Eiffel's structural marvel was now available to all who dared, and Sullivan urged that it be seized and used to change, forever, the Chicago skyline.

Others, including the firm of McKim, Mead, and White, where Bacon worked, advocated a new traditionalism, architecture based on the traditional Victorian style but with greater attention to fully understanding and replicating the spirit of classic Greece and Rome - the Neo-classicism. They rejected the modern movement which they classified as vulgar. Young Henry Bacon would influence the outcome of this conflict.

With their new Classicist focus, Stanford White and Charles F. McKim would go on to provide an image of civic order not seen since ancient Rome. They had just won the commission for the Boston Public Library, orders piled up, and the staff was growing. Into this scenario stepped the cool and confident architect-to-be, Henry Bacon.

In 1889, after less than a year with the firm, Bacon left the firm to accept the Rotch Traveling Scholarship. This scholarship, for a full two years of study and travel in Europe, was the goal he had been pursuing since leaving college, four years before. When the time came to apply, Bacon was already recognized by his peers for his outstanding promise. His win was a foregone conclusion since other candidates, on learning that Bacon was entering, decided not to compete.

On May 22, 1889 Bacon sailed for Europe accompanied by his friend James Brite. His first stop was in Paris. Bacon considered entering the Icole des Beaux-Arts for his two-year period, but decided not to. He did visit the school and stayed in the city for about six months studying the architecture and doing sketches. From there he went to Italy and then on to Greece. Bacon was very impressed with the bold simplicity of the Greeks. Bacon filled pages of his sketchbook with drawings of details and motifs that caught his attention.

Bacon returned to the States in the fall of 1891 and rejoined McKim, Mead and White. As was the custom for returning Rotch scholars, he displayed his drawings at Boston Architectural Club. *Boston Times* critics found Bacon's sketches the best ever produced by a Rotch scholar. His exhibition was so popular that it traveled to Washington and to New York as well. McKim made Bacon his assistant and put him in charge of the design of the Rhode Island Statehouse. Then in May 1892, in the middle of this work, McKim pulled him from the project and loaned him to Daniel Burnham to assist in preparing for the Chicago World's Fair of 1893, the Colombian Exposition.

The controversy over the future direction of American architecture, classicism or modernism, still raged. In Chicago and the mid-west, Sullivan and his followers advocated a revolutionary change in American architecture, a move toward the new modernism coupled with an exploitation of new technology and materials. Meanwhile, the established traditionalists, headed by McKim, Mead and White in New York, were modifying older

Romo-Grecian styles to design even more minimalist structures in the classic style. The traditionalists had two advantages. They had better backing since both government and the capitalistic moguls were conservative and sought and supported the traditionalist architect. Also, they had Daniel Burnham.

Named Chief of Construction of the Fair, Burnham was a leader of the Chicago modernist school. He designed the steel-framed Reliance Building after the principles lain out by Sullivan. Ironically, however, his vision for the Fair included a vast "court of honor" surrounding a lagoon and flanked by monumental buildings, all done in the classical style. The architects chosen included McKim, Mead and White, Hunt, and Charles Atwood. Of these, the most influential was McKim whose personal representative, Henry Bacon, a natural Classicist, was already at Burnham's side. When the Fair opened in 1893, the result was the "White City" a tremendous affirmation of traditional classicism. As a consequence, America entered the new century newly committed to the old ways, while architecture in the rest of the world was exploring new eclectic, art deco, and naturalistic themes. Indeed, some went so far as to suggest that the Fair set architectural progress in America back a hundred years.

Following the Fair, Bacon took a vacation. During his scholarship tour of Europe, he had met Laura Calvert, the sister of his brother's wife and daughter of the British Consul to the Dardanelles. Since his earlier visit, he and Laura had become engaged. Now, Bacon traveled back to Turkey and they were married. After the ceremony, Laura accompanied him to New York.

Bacon's assignments during the next few years were varied, but already he was beginning to work on monuments and memorials. During this period he worked with Augustus St. Gaudens to design the famous Robert Gould Shaw Memorial to the Union Dead in Boston. In interesting counterpoint, working with New York sculptor, F. H. Packer, Bacon later designed the Monument to the Confederate Soldier in Wilmington, North Carolina.

Then, in 1897, Bacon quit McKim, Mead and White and went into partnership with his friend, Jimmy Brite. The Brite and Bacon partnership endured less than six years and, in 1903, the two split up. The cause of the break is not known, but Brite, hampered by health problems, was often absent from work. It seems doubtful that anyone could have matched Bacon 's stolid persistence and dedication to every detail of every task, and possibly the mismatch led to the separation. After the breakup and for the remainder of his life, Bacon worked alone.

Henry Bacon became well known for his design of public build-ings, from libraries and post offices, to the state capital in Providence, Rhode Island, and for his many buildings on campuses. In these, he applied his own interpretation of a Grecian or classical style to create images of stability and civic order. A sense of Bacon's strong, unbending character and his care in harmonizing his work with the surroundings can be felt in these stone structures. His design of the Philadelphia Museum of Art won acclaim for its clean lines and the blending of classic and Federal styles. He also designed large commercial structures such as train stations and office buildings, adopting new techniques and materials for special concerns like large roof spans. The Union Square Savings Bank in New York and the Halle Brothers Department Store in Cleveland Ohio are two of his finer and better-known works. The largest grouping of Bacon's work is found at Wesleyan University, in Connecticut, where he built or renovated a large number of the campus buildings.

Bacon earned a reputation for his attention to detail and his refusal to vary from what he felt was the correct approach, traits that probably grew from his experiences watching his father on the Cape Fear River. This is illustrated in a story about Bacon that was told by Royal Cortissoz, the architectural critic for the *New York Times*:

> Bacon was asked to design a fraternity house. He made the plans, and when the committee was through pouring over them they said they wanted big plate glass windows. The plan called for small panes and this, the committee said, would have to be changed. Bacon said, "It is necessary to the integrity of my design that the panes should be small. If you must have them large the affair is very simple. Give me back my plans, employ someone else and we'll call that little matter settled."

The panes went in small.

A significant portion of Bacon's work, however, consisted of monuments and memorials. More than anything else, Henry Bacon was a great monument architect. In designing scores of monument projects, Henry Bacon focused on the design of the settings and the interrelationship between them, the sculpture, and the surrounding environment. Each memorial had its own setting and was unique, and for each, Bacon used his stone to create a sense of permanence and completeness to the piece.

Bacon developed a rare appreciation of the interdependency of multiple disciplines in a monument or memorial project. He was a master of composition, an artist in his great blocks of stone. In the words of the New York Daily Tribune, "He (Bacon) is a monument architect." When it became time to select an architect for a monument to Lincoln, Bacon would be an obvious contender.

Abraham Lincoln is one of the most beloved of the men who have served as President of the United States and, in 1867, the U.S. Congress decided that a monument should be erected to honor him and created a Monument Association to plan a suitable memorial. For over three decades, while Bacon grew and became a respected architect, no progress was made. Then, in 1900, the Senate Park Commission, known as the McMillan Commission, presented a plan to re-draw the city of Washington. The plan included a memorial to Lincoln.

In the period after 1882, the Potomac River and Washington Navigation Channel had been dredged extensively. Over two million cubic yards of fill were deposited in the marsh and mud flats south and southwest of the White House. Aimed primarily at improving navigation, the fill was expected to have a secondary benefit of reducing the malarial flats and the danger to the city's health. It turned out that there was a third benefit. Over 700 acres of new land had been created west of the Washington Monument.

The McMillan Commissioners envisioned this park as an extension of the Mall, which then terminated at the Washington Monument. Thus a strategic decision was made to extend the formal axis of the Mall to the river, anchor it at a <u>rond-point</u> at the west end, with a strong terminal feature. From this circle, a bridge would be constructed over the river and connecting to Virginia just in front of the National Cemetery, below Arlington House. The Commission saw this connection as important, linking Potomac Park and the Mall into the proposed national park system. Although the circle was a logical location for the Lincoln Memorial, competing factions and alternative ideas delayed the final decision another twelve years.

In 1910, the National Commission of Fine Arts was created and was given authority over nearly all questions of architecture and monuments in Washington DC. A year later the McMillan Commission and the Fine Arts Commission met to decide on a site and design for a memorial to Lincoln, but they couldn't reach a decision. At an impasse, they agreed to hire an architect to help them. The Fine Arts Commission retired from the joint meeting to consider who to select and unanimously recommended Henry Bacon. His selection was not a surprise.

On the technical board of the Arts Commission and advising the decision-making committee was Daniel Burnham, who Bacon worked with on the World's Fair, and Bacon's mentor and former employer, McKim. These two knew Bacon, his rigid, inflexible insistence on excellence in all details, and they knew of his mastery of the architecture of monuments. They convinced the other members of the Commission and Bacon's name was submitted to the Memorial Commission. In the memorandum he prepared to present Bacon's name to the Memorial Commission, Chairman Frank Millet cited Bacon's qualifications. Here was a man that was uniquely qualified, one who had a proven record of outstanding work, and one who was a recognized master in the design of monuments. This wasn't all.

The heart of his recommendation was that Bacon had turned anonymity, reticence, extreme selectivity, and idiosyncratic style into unique advantage. He was the idealist, untainted by all the foregone bickering.

Everyone assumed that the selection of Bacon and the site was final, but there were further attempts to resurrect alternatives. Finally, in February 1912, the Memorial Commission formally selected the Potomac Park site. They surprised everyone, however, by asking both Bacon and John Russell Pope to submit designs for that site. Bacon submitted his new plan on March 28, and Pope presented his the next day. The Commission dithered but, on April 16, 1912, the issue was brought to a vote and Bacon won the right to design the Lincoln Memorial.

Following the announcement of his appointment, a reporter asked Bacon whether the memorial would be purely symbolic or if it would have some utility. Bacon explained his concept: "...it would have no secular uses whatever. Yes, in that one respect it will be like Grant's Tomb, for its significance will be as a memorial to the memory and achievements of Abraham Lincoln." He compared his plan with that of the Parthenon, built by Greek Athenians to house the statue of their goddess, Athenae. He then expressed some of the problems that he would have to consider in the design. "The contiguity with the Washington Obelisk, rising 550 feet into the sky precludes all thought of a structure vying with that in loftiness," he said. "Therefore, horizontal lines are clearly indicated, the colonnaded grandeur of a temple rather than the heaven piercing spires of the Goth, or the towers of the Romanesque." Bacon stressed the need to fit the memorial into the greater architectural scheme, the procession sweeping from the dominating

Capital, around the Mall and even across the river connecting with the Arlington Cemetery. Precise siting and scale were important, he said. "The treatment of the natural surroundings - the frame of the picture - is almost as important as the architecture itself; and last arises the highly interesting question what parts the sister arts of sculpture and painting shall contribute to the embellishment of the exterior and interior."

Bacon's decision to divide the memorial into three chambers was rooted in his choice of the Greek temple as a model. He was, however, faced with a problem no Greek had faced - what to do with the two side chambers. He decided to use the Gettysburg Address on a tablet on one wall, but he needed something equivalent for the opposite side. For this he chose Lincoln's Second Inaugural Address.

It was critical to Bacon's design that the memorial appear to be resting on a hilltop, high above the surrounding land. To accomplish this, he proposed to construct the Memorial high in the air, supported by heavy concrete piers. Afterward, fill would be added to create the illusion of a hilltop, and wide staircases constructed descending from all four sides. Fortunately, over the past few years, the Corps of Engineers had cooperated with the McMillan Commission and had added dredged fill raising most of the area of the memorial above water level. At least Bacon didn't have to start below water.

On December 4, 1912, Bacon's design for the memorial was approved, and he was put in complete charge of the entire project; the design, construction, selection of sculptor, painter, and even the stone cutters. Bacon wrote:

> The most important object is the statue of
> Lincoln. By virtue of its imposing position in the
> place of honor, the gentleness, power, and intelli-
> gence of the man, expressed as far as possible by
> the sculptor's art, predominate.

Bacon knew that his friend, Daniel Chester French would be the perfect artist for the challenge. The Commission agreed. French's first sug-gestion was a standing figure of Lincoln, but Bacon firmly rejected this, feeling that it would not work next to the facade of columns. French then proposed a seated Lincoln statue. This would not be Lincoln, the conquer-ing hero, but a pensive, sorrowful, compassionate man who longed to unite the nation following the Civil War. Bacon agreed.

Bacon selected all of his collaborators with care - artists that he knew and trusted. In addition to French, his sculptor, he chose Jules Guerin to paint the murals, and Royal Cortissoz to carve the inscriptions. He hired his nephew and namesake, Henry Bacon McKoy, to oversee the quarrying. The Piccarilli Brothers of New York prepared the pieces. With his team selected, Bacon was ready to begin work on this, his finest and grandest memorial.

The ground-breaking ceremony for the Lincoln Memorial was held on February 12, 1915, Lincoln's 106th birthday. A heavily bundled President Taft braved the bitter cold of that morning to turn the first shovel full of dirt and construction crews went to work on the building. The first battles came soon after.

Bacon's plans called for the memorial to be supported by rock pil-ings set on the underlying bedrock. The Corps of Engineers objected, holding that a simpler footing designed to spread the load would be much cheaper and would suffice. Bacon did not agree, but didn't argue. It is easy to believe that he would have considered it beneath his station to do so. He had firmly stated his position and was over-ruled. He made note of his objection and work continued until the structure began to settle in the soft soils of the reclaimed land. Bacon 's only comment was "The decision to reject my design cost us a year and wasted many dollars in completing this project." Bacon allowed no more shortcuts on his Memorial.

With proof that he was correct in his belief that the marshy ground wouldn't support the Memrial, Bacon returned to his original plan. Digging down as much as 65 feet to reach bedrock, the work crews constructed a sub-foundation of 122 reinforced concrete piers to create a solid base close to the ground's surface. On top of these came the foundation, a series of long concrete piers 45 feet thick that supported the foundation surface high above the ground. As the great structure rose out of the ground it looked strange with its base, the massive round piers, reaching up into the air. Retaining walls were erected around the structure and along the riverfront and formed the surfaces to support the plaza and steps. Fill was added around the exterior to create the "hill." The floor of the Memorial was placed atop the piers.

Henry Bacon made weekly trips from his home in New York to Washington to oversee the project. For the plaza walls and steps, he chose granite, and for the outer walls and colonnade, white marble from Colorado. Blocks of pink marble from Tennessee formed the floor and for the interior walls and columns he used Indiana limestone. The ceilings were of fine marble panels from Alabama.

This was the commission of dreams, but Bacon complained about the attempts to interfere with his plan, and about the refusals to pay his travel expenses. He had no more trouble with the Corps of Engineers, but others came, including McKim who was designing the Memorial Bridge and proposed a high level span over the river. His lesson learned, Bacon stood fast, insisting that it must be a level crossing and demonstrating how this also helped the circular approaches. McKim was converted. Bacon was equally obstinate with the President of the US when Harding requested changing the inscription behind the seated Lincoln. Bacon refused and the text that he selected endures.

IN THIS TEMPLE
AS IN THE HEARTS OF THE PEOPLE
FOR WHOM HE SAVED THIS NATION
THE MEMORY OF ABRAHAM LINCOLN
IS ENSHRINED FOREVER

As seasons changed the work went on and the structure took form. It faced east with a tall opening behind the colonnade. There was the large center chamber, which would house the Lincoln statue. The south chamber was for the Gettysburg Address and the north for the Second Inaugural Address. Each would be decorated with murals by Jules Guerin; one over the Gettysburg speech depicting Emancipation, and one over the Inaugural Address signifying Reunification. Both murals would feature the Angel of Truth, granting freedom to slaves in the south chamber, and joining the hands of figures representing the North and the South in the north chamber. As the form of the structure evolved, Bacon's artistry became more and more apparent.   He wrote on one of his plans:

> At the time of Lincoln's death there were 36 states (according to the World Almanac) that had been admitted to the Union counting the 13 original thirteen [sic] States. It is a curious coincidence that I happened to draw 36 col's around the building without counting them though I had an idea after making the drawing of having them represent the States. At that time I didn't know the number of states at the close of the War. /H. Bacon.

That the number of columns was a coincidence was later confirmed by William Partridge who wrote:

> That the number of columns in that encircling, 36, meant anything at all is purely coincidental. Henry Bacon cared more for proportion than for recording in columns the number of States in the Union at the time of Lincoln's death..

Having discovered this coincidence early, however, Bacon took advantage of it. He added to the analogy of the 36 columns, making the stairway up the platform of thirteen steps, signifying the original 13 States whose names are carved into the steps of the east front. Over each   column he placed a pair of intertwining wreaths signifying reunion, instead of the normal single wreath. Around the attic he included the names of the forty-eight states that were then members of the Union. Above the colonnade Bacon placed 48 memorial festoons, arranged in groups of three, and supported by eagles. The 36 exterior columns slanted somewhat inwards at the top to provide the illusion of a more stable structure. Long, wide stairway approaches and carefully located tree plantings around the perimeter provided a feeling of isolation and serenity. The effect was better than even he could have anticipated. The quiet, serene atmosphere, which he had sought, was made reality. It was his dream come true.

On May 30, 1922, more than seven years after the groundbreaking ceremony, 50,000 people gathered for the dedication of the Lincoln Memorial. Thanks to a recent invention, the loudspeakers mounted at the corners of the memorial roof, all could hear the speeches. The conveyances also bespoke the new era as rows of parked automobiles stood in the background. Another recent technology advance, radio, made it possible for hundreds of thousands more to listen in at home. Many of them might have wondered about a strange noise in the background, a circling aeroplane, taking photographs of the event.

Since then, the Lincoln Memorial has served many times as the setting for gatherings of Americans seeking to reinforce the ideals embodied in this temple. One of the transcendental events in the civil rights movement occurred there on Easter Sunday in 1939. After opera singer Marian Anderson was denied permission to perform in the segregated Constitution Hall of the DAR, she was invited by Eleanor Roosevelt to give her concert on the steps of the Memorial. Over 75,000 attended that concert of hymns and anthems. In 1963, more than 200,000 crowded about the Memorial as the Reverend Martin Luther King, Jr. proclaimed, "I have a dream." Today, the Lincoln Memorial is still America's most revered national monument. It is open twenty-four hours a day, every day of the year.

Although he maintained his stately calm and appeared, as always, in complete control, Bacon must have found his work on the Memorial extremely difficult. He worked on the Lincoln Memorial over an eleven-year period while keeping his normal business in full operation. Steadfastly independent, he did this alone, splitting his time between projects, weighing and choosing where he should go next, how long to stay, how he could be most effective. Often alone and neglected at home, his wife spent long periods overseas, visiting her family. The only outward indication of the stress Bacon felt was expressed in his sharp reply to McKim who commented about his profit on the Lincoln Memorial. Bacon wrote:

> The reports of my fee being $150,000 are in error. I stand
> to receive a total fee of somewhat less than $40,000
> which will scarce cover my out of pocket and travel
> expenses over these trying years. If I were to be offered
> another commission for the government in
> Washington I doubt that I should accept it.

During his career, Bacon maintained close ties with his family and his hometown of Wilmington. After he received the award from President Harding at the ceremony on the Mall, he returned to North Carolina and spent the holidays there with friends and family. Shortly after his return to New York he became ill. In February 1924, he entered the hospital for an intestinal cancer operation and died a few days later. At the funeral service the pastor drew a parallel between the Lincoln Memorial and its architect, Henry Bacon. He said, "Its dignity, its majesty and its beauty make one of his friends, perhaps all of them, think of the rectitude, of the strength, of that honor and sincerity which richly endowed his nature."

West of Princess Street in a historic section of Wilmington, North Carolina, is Oakdale Cemetery. Stately, dignified, and serenely pastoral, the gravestones are surrounded by azaleas that blossom brilliant hues in spring. They are sheltered from the heat of summer sun by stately trees, live oaks and cherries that arch overhead. There is an inscription carved on a marble bench here that seems appropriate; "A tree is known by its fruits, and the noble family by a nobleman."

Here also is the Bacon family plot. In February 1924, in a quiet dignified ceremony, Henry Bacon, Jr. was laid to rest here, next to his parents and brothers. His grave marker was designed from his drawing of an ancient grave *stele* from Greece. It is inscribed simply,

HENRY BACON

1866-1924

THE ARCHITECT OF THE LINCOLN MEMORIAL

AT WASHINGTON, D.C.